America's Game
Atlanta Braves

CHRIS W. SEHNERT

ABDO & Daughters
PUBLISHING

Published by Abdo & Daughters, 4940 Viking Dr., Suite 622, Edina, MN 55435.

Cover photo: Allsport
Interior photos: Wide World Photo, pages 1, 5, 9, 12, 13, 15, 17, 21-28.

Edited by Paul Joseph

Library of Congress Cataloging–in–Publication Data

Sehnert, Chris W.
   Atlanta Braves / Chris W. Sehnert
      p. cm. — (America's game)
   Includes index.
   Summary: An account of the baseball team's history representing three cities before arriving in Atlanta in 1966 and ultimately winning the World Championship there in 1995.
   ISBN 1-56239-663-3
   1. Atlanta Braves (Baseball team)—History—Juvenile literature.
[1. Atlanta Braves (Baseball team)—History 2. Baseball—History.]
I. Title. II. Series.
GV875.A8S45 1997
796.357'64'09758231—dc20   96-2372
                                      CIP
                                      AC

Contents

Atlanta Braves

The history of the Atlanta Braves baseball team is a tale of four cities. The Braves' great-grandfather organization was the Cincinnati Red Stockings, the first club to play baseball professionally. In 1871, Harry Wright moved his Red Stockings to Boston, where they became founding members of baseball's first professional league, the National Association (NA).

The team played 81 seasons in Boston, while going through several name changes. The Red Stockings became the Beaneaters, then were known as the Doves, Rustlers, and Bees, before settling on the Boston Braves.

The Braves moved to Milwaukee in 1953. One year later, a rookie named Henry Aaron began his incredible, record-setting career. After 13 seasons and a World Championship, the Braves headed south to their current home in Atlanta, Georgia.

In the 1990s, the Atlanta Braves became the most dominant team in the National League (NL). Their pitching staff of "Young Guns" carried the team to five division titles, four NL Pennants, and the 1995 World Championship!

Braves' sluggers David Justice and Fred McGriff are on a pace that could land them on the list of all-time greats. Meanwhile, Greg Maddux has been the NL's top pitcher four-straight times. The current generation of Atlanta Braves are proud members of baseball's oldest ancestry.

Atlanta Braves' righthander
Greg Maddux delivers a pitch.

Baseball's First Dynasty

Back in 1869, Harry Wright organized the Cincinnati Red Stockings and brought them on a tour. They played the best amateur baseball clubs in North America, and became the first team to openly charge admission and pay their players.

The Red Stockings went undefeated in their first season, winning some 60 games in a row. The next year, they won their first 24 games before being knocked off by the Brooklyn Atlantics in 11 innings.

Before the opening of the 1871 baseball season, leaders from a group of the nation's best amateur clubs gathered for a meeting. In one evening, they created the National Association (NA). Major League Baseball had begun.

The Cincinnati ballclub had already voted to return to the amateur ranks. Wright took his star players and moved them to Boston, Massachusetts, where they joined the new league. Wright also kept the team's name.

Among the Red Stockings who made the trip to Boston was George Wright. Harry's younger brother was the team's star shortstop. The Wright brothers were joined by pitcher Al Spalding before the NA's inaugural season. All three would later be inducted into the Baseball Hall of Fame.

Baseball's first major league lasted five years (1871-1875). Spalding was the league's top pitcher in all five. The Red Stockings finished a close second to the Philadelphia Athletics in 1871. The next four NA Pennants were all taken by Boston.

The Boston Red Stockings were Major League Baseball's first dynasty. They were broken up in 1876, when Al Spalding was lured to the Chicago White Stockings (the original Cubs). That was the first season of the new National League (NL).

The Wright brothers remained in Boston, where the Red Stockings acquired Tommy Bond before the 1877 season. Bond became the first major leaguer to achieve a pitching Triple Crown that year, leading the NL in wins, strikeouts, and earned run average (ERA). He matched his victory total (40) in 1878, as Boston became NL Champions both years.

Beaneaters

The departure of the Wright brothers signaled the end of an era for the team known today as the Braves. The Red Stockings, led by the pitching of "Grasshopper Jim" Whitney, took one more NL Pennant in 1883, before dropping off in the standings for the remainder of the decade.

In 1890, the organization changed its name to the Boston Beaneaters, and embarked on a second era of greatness. The Beaneaters hired Frank Selee to manage the team, after he had led his Omaha ballclub to minor league pennants two-straight times. Selee brought Omaha's pitching ace, Charles "Kid" Nichols, along with him to Boston.

At 20 years old, Kid was an immediate success. Nichols led the NL in shutouts with seven in his rookie season. He followed by leading the Beaneaters to five NL Pennants in the next eight years.

The Beaneaters returned to win two more NL Pennants before 1900 (1897 and 1898). In the 29 years of 19th century Major League Baseball, Boston won 12 championships.

The 1914 Boston Braves' Miracle Team.

Miracle Braves

The 20th century ushered in Major League Baseball's modern era. By 1901, the American League (AL) was considered equal to the "Senior Circuit" of the NL on a competitive level. The rival leagues began World Series play in 1903.

The Beaneaters now had a rivalry of their own, just across town. The Boston Pilgrims (the original Red Sox), led by their pitcher, Cy Young, were among the best teams in the new league. The Pilgrims won the 1903 AL Pennant and defeated Pittsburgh in the first World Series. The Beaneaters, meanwhile, suffered through their worst season in 20 years.

Boston's downward spiral in the NL standings coincided with a number of name changes for the team. Between 1909 and 1912, whether known as the Beaneaters, Doves, Rustlers, or Braves, one thing remained consistent: They finished in last place every year.

After recovering slightly in the previous season, the 1914 Boston Braves looked to be heading back to the NL cellar. But with a new lineup that featured veteran second baseman Johnny Evers and third-year shortstop Walter "Rabbit" Maranville, the Braves began to turn things around in mid-season. The Braves suddenly became a team to contend with, winning 9 out of 12 games to escape last place on July 19th.

The miraculous Braves hosted the powerful New York Giants in a battle for first place during early September. The Braves took two out of three and never looked back, winning the 1914 NL Pennant by 10.5 games.

Boston's stretch-drive that season remains the greatest in baseball history (68-19). They carried their winning ways into Philadelphia, where they met the Athletics in the World Series. With four-straight victories, the "Miracle Braves" became the 1914 World Champions.

Spahn and Sain

The Braves continued their league-leading fielding for two years after their 1914 World Championship season. Boston's pitching, meanwhile, fell off sharply, and Rabbit Maranville was traded to the Pittsburgh Pirates in 1921.

The following season, the Braves were back in last place. For two decades, while the New York Giants and St. Louis Cardinals were dominating the NL, the Boston Braves consistently occupied the bottom of the standings.

Casey Stengel took over as manager in 1938. After four more unsuccessful campaigns, the Braves promoted two young pitchers to the big league club in 1942.

Right-hander Johnny Sain completed the season in Boston, appearing mostly in relief. Warren Spahn was sent back to the minors when he failed to obey Stengel's order to throw a brush-back pitch. The next season, both players were taking orders of a different kind. They were serving military duty for the United States in World War II.

Spahn and Sain returned to join Boston's starting rotation in 1946. They each had 21 wins in 1947. Third baseman Bob Elliott was named the 1947 NL Most Valuable Player (MVP), combining powerful hitting with his league-leading defensive play.

In 1948, the Boston Braves put it together, taking the NL Pennant by 6.5 games over the St. Louis Cardinals. Shortstop Alvin Dark was named Rookie of the Year. He was among five regulars in the

Braves' lineup with a batting average above .300. Johnny Sain led the NL in wins with 24, while many of Warren Spahn's 15 victories came during the crucial September stretch drive.

Spahn and Sain each picked up one more victory in the 1948 World Series, but it wasn't enough as the Cleveland Indians won the World Championship in six games.

Johnny Sain had his fourth 20-win season for the Braves in 1950. The following year he was traded to the New York Yankees, where his playing career took a sharp decline. He later became known as one of the greatest pitching coaches of all time. Warren Spahn remained with the Braves, traveling with the team to their new home in Milwaukee, Wisconsin.

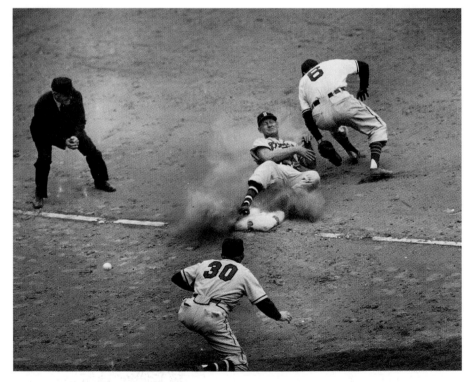

Above: Bob Elliott slides safely into third base in the seventh inning of Game 5 of the 1948 World Series against the Cleveland Indians.

Facing Page: Warren Spahn warms up before a game.

Milwaukee Braves

The city of Boston has been one of America's great baseball towns for as long as the game has been played. By the late 1940s, however, the Braves organization was finding it difficult to compete in an area which had two major league teams.

In 1948, the year the Boston Braves won their final NL Pennant, the Boston Red Sox attracted more fans. Three years later, Braves' attendance hit a five-year low for any NL ballclub. In an effort to survive, Braves' ownership moved the team to Milwaukee in 1953, where they were welcomed with open arms.

The Milwaukee Braves set an all-time NL attendance record in their first season. The next year, they became the first NL club to draw over two million fans! Some of those two million witnessed a rookie, Henry Louis Aaron, Jr., hit his first major league home run.

Aaron came to the Braves from the Negro League. "Hammerin' Hank's" talents were clearly evident, and in 1954 he became one more superstar in a powerful Milwaukee lineup.

Eddie Mathews was the Braves' third baseman. He won the NL's home run crown with 47 in 1953.

Warren Spahn was in the midst of becoming the winningest left-handed pitcher of all time. He led the NL in wins with 23 for the third time in 1953.

Facing page: "Hammerin' Hank" Aaron in 1961.

The Braves finished the year just one game behind the Brooklyn Dodgers in the 1956 NL Pennant race. The following year, Milwaukee became the team to beat.

The Braves acquired veteran second baseman Red Schoendienst from the New York Giants to shore up the defense in 1957. Schoendienst, a future Hall of Famer, led the NL in hits with 200 that season, setting the table for Mathews and Aaron.

Hank Aaron's 44 home runs matched his famous uniform number, and along with his 132 RBIs, he was the NL's leader in both categories. Warren Spahn's 21 wins earned him the Cy Young Award, and began a string of 5 consecutive seasons in which he led the league in victories.

The Braves took the 1957 NL Pennant by eight games over the St. Louis Cardinals. They faced Casey Stengel's New York Yankees in the World Series.

Lew Burdette pitched three complete game victories for the Braves in the Series. Spahn picked up the other Braves victory, with a 10-inning performance in Game 4. Burdette threw his second shutout of the Series in Game 7, as the Milwaukee Braves became the 1957 World Champions.

The following season ended with a rematch in the Fall Classic. Milwaukee jumped out to an early Series lead of three games to one. However the Yankees won the final three games and regained their World Champion status.

The Braves continued to field winning teams in Milwaukee for the next seven seasons. They finished second twice, but never won another pennant.

Whether they were spoiled by success, or the novelty had worn off, Braves' fans were attending fewer ballgames. Attendance at Milwaukee's County Stadium began a steady decline in 1958. By 1962, it had dropped below one million fans. The Braves tried another city, moving to Atlanta, Georgia, in 1966.

Hank Aaron hammers one over the outfield fence.

Oh Henry!

Growing up in Mobile, Alabama, young Henry Aaron taught himself to hit by swinging a broom handle at bottle caps. He later credited this experience for his ability to react to a breaking ball at the last possible second. The experience of being raised in a racially segregated country drove him to chase Babe Ruth's "unbreakable" record.

Aaron signed a contract with the Braves in 1952, just five years after Jackie Robinson broke Major League Baseball's "color barrier." Both players would set new standards for the game, while facing rampant discrimination.

 17

Atlanta

Third baseman Bob Elliott was named the 1947 NL MVP.

Warren Spahn pitched for the Braves during the 1948 World Series against the Cleveland Indians.

Henry Aaron finished his major league career in 1976 with 755 home runs and 2,297 RBIs.

Pitcher Phil Niekro led the NL in 1974 with 20 wins.

Braves

Dale Murphy was the NL MVP in both 1982 and 1983.

In 1991, Pitcher Tom Glavine took the NL Cy Young Award.

In his first season with the Braves, Terry Pendleton was named the 1991 NL MVP.

Outfielder David Justice won the 1990 NL Rookie of the Year Award.

By the time the Braves moved to Atlanta in 1966, Hank already had 2 batting crowns, 3 RBI crowns, and 398 career home runs. For some reason, his achievements had gone largely unnoticed by the media. He continued his assault on NL pitching with home run crowns in 1967 and 1968.

The Atlanta Braves won the 1969 NL West in the first year of divisional play. They were swept by New York's "Miracle Mets" in the National League Championship Series (NLCS). "Hammerin' Hank" homered in all three games.

In 1970, Henry Aaron became the ninth player in major league history to reach 3,000 hits. He was also the first African-American on the list. The following season, at the age of 37, Aaron hit a career high 47 home runs.

Babe Ruth finished his career with 714 home runs. Aaron's 40 home runs in 1973 left him one behind the "sacred" mark.

In his first at-bat of the 1974 season, Aaron cranked number 714. Three games later, he hit the record-breaker, number 715.

Aaron ended his career in the town where he played his rookie season. He hit 22 home runs as a Milwaukee Brewer, and retired in 1976.

Henry Aaron finished his career as Major League Baseball's all-time leader in both home runs, with 755, and RBIs, with 2,297. He is tied with Babe Ruth for second on the all-time runs list with 2,174, and ranks third in hits with 3,771. "Hammerin' Hank" Aaron joined the Baseball Hall of Fame in 1982.

Ted's Team

Outside of Henry Aaron's heroics, Atlanta baseball fans were left with little to cheer about in the early 1970s. Phil Niekro was the ace of the Braves' pitching staff. His younger brother, Joe Niekro, was also a pitcher. The Niekro brothers were masters of the knuckleball. Together, they have more wins than any brotherly combination in major league history.

In 1974, Phil led the NL with 20 wins, while Joe pitched out of Atlanta's bullpen. The team continued to struggle. However, in 1976, the Braves were sold to a millionaire businessman named Ted Turner.

Turner was a pioneer of the cable television industry. He used the Braves to draw a nationwide audience to his new television "SuperStation," WTBS.

Below: The view from home plate when Phil Niekro throws one of his famous knuckleballs.

Atlanta Braves' outfielder Dale Murphy.

The Braves finally turned the corner and won the NL West Title in 1982. They were led by the NL's MVP, Dale Murphy. Murphy played 15 seasons with the Atlanta Braves. He made his only post-season appearance in 1982. The Braves were swept in the NLCS by the St. Louis Cardinals.

Dale Murphy returned to win his second consecutive NL MVP Award in 1983. He won NL home run crowns in 1984 and 1985, was an NL All-Star seven times, and won five Gold Glove Awards.

Worst To First

By 1991, Ted Turner's Cable News Network had become internationally renowned. His baseball team, which finished last in 1990, was also capturing attention. The 1991 Atlanta Braves became the first team in NL history to go from worst to first in one year's time.

The Braves battled the Los Angeles Dodgers in a see-saw race for the NL West Division Title. Attendance at Fulton County Stadium, which had been the lowest in baseball for three-straight seasons, soared beyond the two million mark.

Terry Pendleton heads to first base on a seventh-inning single that scored Jeff Blauser in Game 3 of the 1993 NLCS against the Philadelphia Phillies.

The Braves' offense was powered by third baseman Terry Pendleton. In his first season with Atlanta, Pendleton took the NL batting crown and was named the 1991 NL MVP. His teammates included outfielders David Justice (the 1990 NL Rookie of the Year), and Ron Gant, who produced 30 home runs and 30 stolen bases for the second-straight season.

Tom Glavine took the 1991 NL Cy Young Award, leading a pitching staff known as the "Young Guns." At 25 years old, Glavine was the senior member of a trio that included Steve Avery and John Smoltz. The "Guns" were blazing in the 1991 NLCS, as they shut out the powerful Pittsburgh Pirates three times en route to the NL Pennant.

The 1991 World Series was a true classic. The Minnesota Twins had pulled a worst-to-first turnaround of their own to capture the AL Pennant. The Braves and Twins faced off in a seven-game struggle,

Facing Page: Braves' pitcher John Smoltz winds up for a pitch against the Minnesota Twins during the first inning of Game 7 of the 1991 World Series.
Right: David Justice is greeted by Ron Gant after both scored on Justice's two-run home run in the fourth inning of Game 5 of the 1991 World Series.

filled with outstanding play. Five of the games were decided by one run. Three went into extra innings, including Game 6 and Game 7. The Twins broke a scoreless tie in the 10th inning of the final game to win the World Championship.

The Braves won their second-straight NL Pennant in 1992. This time they were defeated in a six-game World Series by the Toronto Blue Jays. In 1993, Atlanta won its third-straight NL West Division Title, but were defeated by the Philadelphia Phillies in the NLCS.

The Braves added a new "Gun" to their arsenal in 1993. Greg Maddux won the 1992 NL Cy Young Award as a member of the Chicago Cubs. For the next three seasons, he won the award while pitching for Atlanta. Philly Hall-of-Famer Steve Carlton was previously the only pitcher with four Cy Young Awards. Greg Maddux won his fourth in a row at the age of 29.

With the NL realigned into three divisions in 1994, the Braves moved into the NL East. That season was never completed, ending in August due to a players' strike. Play resumed in 1995, and Atlanta won their first NL East Division Championship by 21 games over the Philadelphia Phillies!

Atlanta Braves' starting pitcher Tom Glavine hurls against the Minnesota Twins in Game 5 of the 1991 World Series.

Ron Gant rips a double during the sixth inning of Game 1 of the 1991 World Series against the Minnesota Twins.

The "Young Guns" of Greg Maddux, Tom Glavine, John Smoltz, and Steve Avery provided the Braves with league-leading pitching.

Atlanta defeated the wild card Colorado Rockies in a divisional playoff, before sweeping the Cincinnati Reds in the NLCS. They returned to the World Series for the third time in five years.

The Braves met the Cleveland Indians in the 1995 Fall Classic. In another closely contested matchup, five out of the six games were decided by a single run. Tom Glavine pitched eight innings of the final game, allowing only one hit and no runs. A solo home run hit by David Justice was enough to give Glavine his second win of the Series, and Atlanta its first World Championship.

A Dynasty

The Atlanta Braves continued their winning ways in 1996, making them a true National League dynasty. They easily won their second-straight NL East title and then quickly dismantled the Los Angeles Dodgers in the first round of the playoffs.

The Braves were down three games to one to the St. Louis Cardinals in the NLCS when they turned up the firepower. They scored run after run to come back and claim the National League Pennant.

The Braves kept the power going in the World Series against the New York Yankees. It looked as though the Braves would capture their second-straight World Series, winning Game 1 (12-1) and Game 2 (4-0), both in the Bronx. But the Yankees fought back and stole the World Series, winning the next four-straight games.

The Atlanta Braves have established themselves as the NL's newest dynasty. Their current lineup includes some of the brightest young stars in the major leagues. They are the living legacy of the first professional baseball team.

David Justice watches the ball fly in Game 4 of the 1991 World Series against the Minnesota Twins.

Glossary

All-Star: A player who is voted by fans as the best player at one position in a given year.

American League (AL): An association of baseball teams formed in 1900 which make up one-half of the major leagues.

American League Championship Series (ALCS): A best-of-seven-game playoff with the winner going to the World Series to face the National League Champions.

Batting Average: A baseball statistic calculated by dividing a batter's hits by the number of times at bat.

Earned Run Average (ERA): A baseball statistic which calculates the average number of runs a pitcher gives up per nine innings of work.

Fielding Average: A baseball statistic which calculates a fielder's success rate based on the number of chances the player has to record an out.

Hall of Fame: A memorial for the greatest baseball players of all time located in Cooperstown, New York.

Home Run (HR): A play in baseball where a batter hits the ball over the outfield fence scoring everyone on base as well as the batter.

Major Leagues: The highest ranking associations of professional baseball teams in the world, currently consisting of the American and National Baseball Leagues.

Minor Leagues: A system of professional baseball leagues at levels below Major League Baseball.

National League (NL): An association of baseball teams formed in 1876 which make up one-half of the major leagues.

National League Championship Series (NLCS): A best-of-seven-game playoff with the winner going to the World Series to face the American League Champions.

Pennant: A flag which symbolizes the championship of a professional baseball league.

Pitcher: The player on a baseball team who throws the ball for the batter to hit. The pitcher stands on a mound and pitches the ball toward the strike zone area above the plate.

Plate: The place on a baseball field where a player stands to bat. It is used to determine the width of the strike zone. Forming the point of the diamond-shaped field, it is the final goal a base runner must reach to score a run.

RBI: A baseball statistic standing for *runs batted in.* Players receive an RBI for each run that scores on their hits.

Rookie: A first-year player, especially in a professional sport.

Slugging Percentage: A statistic which points out a player's ability to hit for extra bases by taking the number of total bases hit and dividing it by the number of at bats.

Stolen Base: A play in baseball when a base runner advances to the next base while the pitcher is delivering his pitch.

Strikeout: A play in baseball when a batter is called out for failing to put the ball in play after the pitcher has delivered three strikes.

Triple Crown: A rare accomplishment when a single player finishes a season leading their league in batting average, home runs, and RBIs. A pitcher can win a Triple Crown by leading the league in wins, ERA, and strikeouts.

Walk: A play in baseball when a batter receives four pitches out of the strike zone and is allowed to go to first base.

World Series: The championship of Major League Baseball played since 1903 between the pennant winners from the American and National Leagues.

Index